A [CUPBOARD] FULL OF TOMBOYS

Jay Farley is a non-binary, neurodivergent award winning filmmaker and digital artist. Discovering their Non-binary identity in 2022 aged 48 was profound and they found their voice as a performer and poet. Farley subsequently became award winning with 'I Wish I'd Won the Miners' Strike', published in *How it Started*, Creative Futures Writers' Award 2022 anthology. They are published in the *Queer Icons* anthology, *Sparks*, *Hot Poets* anthology and illustrated in *Woop Woop* magazine. Their debut book of poetry *A [Cupboard] Full of Tomboys* was created under the mentorship of TS.Elliot Award winning Joelle Taylor and published by Broken Sleep Books.

ISBN: 978-1-916938-79-3

Cover designed by Aaron Kent

Cover art by Jay Farley

Edited and Typeset by Aaron Kent

Broken Sleep Books Ltd
PO BOX 102
Llandysul
SA44 9BG

CONTENTS

A [Cupboard] Full of Tomboys

Jay Farley

Broken Sleep Books

FOREWORD

The first part of this book is autobiographical and inward facing: starting with stories from inside a cupboard [closeted]. It is the discovery of the cupboard, the realisation that the poet to be, was in fact in a cupboard, [Non-Binary], and the opening of the cupboard door. This represents a time spanning 40 years, an epoch of not feeling valid or having a place in the world.

The second part looks at the discovery of the strange, joyous, and scary new world outside the cupboard. These 'shape' poems almost feel their form has been preordained or infiltrated by homogeneous, patriarchal, external factors in the wider world. But at the same time the rebellious individual queer voice shines through and they are subverted.

My little doll is hidden, housed and held inside the form of a Matryoshka, a Russian Doll, yet directly confronts misogyny and gender norms. Twitter is my deadname, takes the shape of the Twitter bird which is formed by direct quotes from the platform now renamed [x].

Also, there is a consistent visual convention of referring to the cupboard via block monolithic structures representing patriarchy, authority, confinement, and the enforced Gender Binary - as well as reflecting the binary in 0's and 1's.

The third part of the book is the Heroic Crown of Sonnets and tells the stories of the other adventurers I have met on my new journey, and represents an archival collaborative experience of Gender explorers in the 2020's.

A NOTE ON 'NOT BEING':

Sometimes the poems describe not doing things, of not being, in a way that actually means I did. *I didn't go into a bedroom showroom.* It's not clear if this happened or not. This reflects the state of not feeling valid or real, of language not existing to describe life outside the Gender Binary until recent times in the [West], of there being no visibility, no icons, no history and also politically it refers to the lack of legal recognition for non-binary/Gender Queer/Gender non-conforming people. The Gender Binary is so enforced and so constructed it's hard to understand what is real.

A general note to follow relates to rules of punctuation, which are laid out in the Key below.

Punctuation Key:
(please read this key then forget it)

[ ] = closeted in the cupboard, closed, oppressed, hidden

> = promise, progress movement, journey

< = getting worse

/ = a bit hopeful

\ = a bit negative or alot negative

? = doubt

... =

\Part One\ Inside the Cupboard

BREADCRUMBS

walking >>>

past no mark \ small time \ small town shops | past a bookies, a Jarg KFC \past a closed down half post office\half pound shop half nail salon. Some [weeds] bloke\ing through where the <outsourced> Council Parks and Maintenance had missed a patch of pavement with !Monsanto's Roundup! Then, I [didn't] go into a bedroom showroom and in there, I opened a [cupboard] It was full of tomboys thousands of them all ladded in | They were all there [two Joan's/1 armored/ 1Pope'd up/Vesta/Tiny/Scout/Marlene/Jodie /Frida/Mae/ kate>kae> | Someone> had just chucked them in there <<<and some had just walked in of their own accord / It stunk of sweaty socks / and soil / and climbed trees | With shin pads *1* proud bruises /yer dad's watch/ dungarees / dirty knees / None of them where past 13   years   old
Frozen   in
Time

[[T o m b o y]   T i m e]

little   amber   inclusions =   syruped   in   Lucozade
I asked them   >>>   how they got there Some didn't even know [they] were there ...Some had been lost >some had been looking / For the lost . . .   Football / I saw myself/ In the cupboard /I pulled out my posture it was on hangers \that were meat hooks [JJJ] My gender[boy?[enby]] was sewn into the inside of a donkey jacket in case I lost it but the jacket was too small now and the pockets were filled with space lego people\they spilled

out got under my feet so it was too painful to walk like myself\a missing treasure map marked a mountain to climb\ which had the same contours as my thumbprint\which had the same pattern as my dna\ which was missing \It was written in lemon \ only to be seen if held to sun \ but it was dark in the cupboard \ I tried to find the exact [moment] we got there   [In the cupboard] No one could remember we all amnesia'd somnambulant\ had we been stolen? stashed ? an ambush of hoydens ~ hijacked?   or hibernating\or just liked   cupboards\it\was\all\   blurry

Anyway I   left   the   door   open   >

THE POPPED FOOTBALL

comin home from footie with worth/it pained/frozen hands'n'feet/
Muddy/wet/trainers/chucked/in/the/airing/cupboard/
frosted/wobbly/glass/kitchen/door/window/boiled/cabbage/
steamedup/scoffed   /down/with-the-score/draws-final/score/
distorting/out/the/little//telly/on/top/of/the/wood/effect/hot/
point/fridge/freezer./PARTICK/THISTLE:1/HEARTS/OF/
MID/LOTHIAN:/2/SHEFFIELD/WED/NESDAY:3/QUEENS/
PARK/RA/NGERS:NIL.fillin in the pools/for me mum lads/called
round/ grabbed the footy an out/St.Peys school field/of/dreams/
three'n'in/rush/goalie/keepy/ups/sprawling/summer/matches/
that/lasted/all day with 20/odd on each side/got to play with the
big/lads and aspey's dad once/carrying/on with a heroic/bad/
ankle>till/the/sky/turned/orange>and/my/silhouette   scored/
the/winning/goal>and>they>lifted me/high>and^crowned me\
king^-[back-to-school-after-holidays] [got taken off the\boys\
football\team]\   [[[[[[[[[[Cos I was a girl]]]]]]]]]]]]]
['n' the lads stopped coming round] \ didn't happen overnight   \
\like Alun Smiths moustache \ or zits or[periods] but one bra\
size at< a time < took my eye off\the\ball and panini\sticker\
album turned\into Look\in\magazine \ the football under\the\
bed wasn't popped\it had   just lost   air
over time<

WHAT REALLY GOES DOWN AT THE HAIRDRESSERS
(death by a thousand cuts)

A wave of fragrance \clip\ as I \flick\ through magazines all the faces mock me. I don't belong here, \flick\ The wall to wall mirrors look back at me and agree. Flick\ am I even here? \clip\ (can't reach the basin so I contort myself into bridge to reach the urinaled snip\ neck-sink \snip\.) I don't fancy you, you know, cause you're massaging my head with rapidly alternating scalding and freezing water, I'm not weird? \clip\ Chattering snips warmly in the backroom.Soapy suds and dignity down the plug as I'm conditioned. hairdresser asks what style? \cut\ I don't say "not like a woman or a man, and especially not like a woman, please." and Everyone in the entire salon doesn't swivel round simultaneously to stare and the hairdresser's arms don't extend 3 metres down to reach me as I don't sink into a borehole.

(but her voice, distant now) asks what do you \snip\ do for a job?" "I don't give myself permission to be alive. So, can she even see me?" Does that give you a [not valid] discount? \snip\She doesn't really say, in my imagination, in her head, in my head

I hate customers like this \snip\ it's just awkward. my hair now looks like the pixie cut on page 17, that I actually said I wanted! Then The hair dryer pulled out of its holster \flick\ fatal All ready to do that bit at the end that makes my hair look even more femme \flick\ hot air conversion therapy "I'm blown away by it"

I'm on the floor being brushed to the corners ......Everyone looks more comfortable now As I'm trans\flicking\formed From what seemed like the impossible when I walked in, all ugly\flicking\ duckling,and I, I'm not a swan! I'm in shock, fem feathered

And sprayed that way to stay for up to 24 hours of lasting hold Are they complicit in this counterfeit identity? You can't plead ignorance you know \ I comb the area for a quick exit \ clip\Fighting for my life single handedly \clip\ without a pair of scissors to stand on. \snip\And then, as if that wasn't enough, a mirror to show me the back. There is no-one in the reflection But we both say thanks :) salon stunned, striplight eyed, forged signature smile, so fragile the wind coming through the door with a new customer nearly steals it.

WAITING ON AT THE BURLINGTON (5)

same stale black & whites as yesterday
shades on, getting a backy to The Burlington

going back to The Burlington, shaded
hungover brash and dusk fragile

a brash hangover still dusking
watching time layered plate on plate away

wishing stale time layered plate on tectonic plate shift
work sponge down the stains of last night

last night's stains work me down
yes I am small for the hundredth time

for the hundredth small time man again
I drag up my little black skirt for you

but my little black skirt is drag
you cop a look at my tits my dainty legs

my dainty legs my tits exposed to you
face stuffing your full English

your full English stuffed face
pays for my minimum wage

but it's me that pays in the end
gender is not like my black & white's

my gender is not this black & white
carrying the day falls to my crying feet

I carry crying days in my feet
still waiting on \ living

Playstation at the allotment
plugged into the radishes
Bone china on the middle
lane of M56 Chip butty at
Ritz <Cat at dog show
Football at ballet Hoody at
ball<Three piece suite in
the jungle<yor'eet at'
networking event mongst
canopies<Kindness at cash
machine Reflection in mirror
Awkward at the supermarket
Weakness anywhere <Me
at the Women's toilets at
Sandbach services hesitating
at the door signs Smiling
through the mirror<To the mum
with her kid (If I've taken the
eye contact route) at the soap
dispensers, washing my hands
[just like a woman] or head
down invisible, clandestine op
Shields up, cloaking device on
<a kid that covers their face<
I leave without
<   a trace   <

CHOG AND THE LOST NAME

This Tomboy lost their name on the park path or
the school field or it just washed out in the bath.
They shrugged up to me the other day>tugged at
my leg. 'Have you seen it?'   they said
                                                  'What?'
'I think someone might have pinched it.'
        "Are you sure you didn't just grow out of it?
'No, I never'... So >   we started to look, all over,
In nettles and tall grass, up the thin poplar trees
but things kept disappearing < One time a whole
school just turned to dandelions and bindweed
I said 'can you remember the last time you had it'
'Dunno' sobbing now 'maybe when my mum
called me in for me tea' < their tears started to
wash them away, a salty watercolour.
I tried to paint them back to life but there was a
binary brewing and the wind lifted the poor kid
off the ground.
<   I held on tight.
Landed   about 40 years later,
                  wet and bedragged
the kid gone <   i found a new name > on my jacket

NOT BEEN

not seen

not been\no-one been\has been\

yet to be\no bind, binder,   blinder, blinded\

blended,blender,   bender, bonded,

blinkered. Sinkered.   Sunk.Non valid, hungry,

un heard   Missing in action

from the war on   words, lost cultures

and consonants   buried invisible by

greedy hands, across   Continents dug deep

trowelled vowels   Just unearthed

Growing with   planted feet

Lets meet.   Where've you

been all my life?   Left me to the

dust, dry, desert   of no one,

so thirsty I   could drink

a six pack of you,   mirage hits you over

the head like a brick,   mirror.

sun stunned you   chisel away at it

brick by look.   Waving at all

the people   on the other side.

Not man, not woman,   not valid, not valid,

not seen.   In Between

Not been.

N.B. NEBRASKA!,

Atomic number 4,
no buts, no bins,
no beans? naked body,
no body, nobody, neutral
biology, nice boobs,
neglected breasts,
neurotic behaviour,
not boring, naturally
butch, navy blue,
nuerodiverse brain,
name banned, newly
battered, new blood,
nail biting, night baddie,
nightmare bullies, never
being, nervous breakdown,
nuclear bomb, nostalgically
brave, nihilistic bravado,
nausea bucket, no bullshit,
no borders, nature bucked,
natural being, nuanced
behaviour, now breathe,
now breathe, now breathe,
NewBorn,N.b. Nota bene,
Non-Binary.

I \ MISSING WORDS THEY\ GHAZAL

We've been erased by the lack of them
We've been stabbed, written in the back by [words]

We've been edited \ hemorrhaging swaggers
Since the Binary Boats drank our words

We've been lettered & left limp ladies by the theft
We've been stripped speechless, bereft of words

Sank and double drowned   deleted
Dewitched, despatched and dyked by words

We've been curtseyed characters crafted cute
Girl-ied\gracefully\through\the\grapevine\of\words

Lives Abridged stolen bare
vowled to vanishing by words

Whispered till wenches
Scripted senseless by words

heckled hens herded by histories
Been paraphrased \ pecked politely by words

We've been spread thinly across toasts
hipped hungry for words

I've waited 40 years

Epoched   by   words

Life on mute, A forty stretch

But now after my 40, I'm resurrected   by >words>

II FOUND WORDS /THEM GHAZAL VERSION 2

Dazzled by sun /staggering /transported /found/
Strut / wagging / all dog before walk

    All Hollywood yawns /discovered/
    A good self-conscious/gives me the nod

        In a shop window/I'm there!
        Reflection delivers a smile

            And together/we open it/
            Butching down the street

                bouncing to my own /noted/ beat
                Dusting down thirsty thoughts

                    Looking /them/ right in
                the eye/I see them/
                    I have /them/ my words

                Because i am / the words
                I hold them tight/ honeyed
        handsome/ I write /them/

            Shout/ sing/ spit/ and spill /them/
            push them through letterboxes

      sneak them onto to people's shopping lists
      Finish people's crosswords with /them/

Tag bus seats with /them/
Message them in bottles

get pissed on /them/
And wake up next to /them/

AFTER ANDRE BAGOO + THOM GUNN

One night, No-one
+ nowhere,
They had
woken
Decided to travel
Westward of West
Fall to the ocean. Where it led
They would go = They traveled
emptier of the things they knew.
ran away empty, Fell emptier=Shedding
Themselves with each footprint + Skin to earth
Cliff face memories eroding into   sea
as They become less   Her   more dirt/more Them
less

-

Less
Can you subtract   -   what's not there?
The sand and soil blows Them lighter/   Through Them
in between the toes of Them/ Sun baked wind grown
Steel skies cloud them clean+wash/Before /away
But if They stand still   long enough
They'll take root Again and Dissolve into
the   Last Mountain
So They keep moving. The path
bites time at Their heals and
Their skin is caked with

Road Still trying to
shed that load

WOMAN

I

What do I do with the woman.
Does [she] step politely into the 6ft hole
like a bath one leg at a time
from where I dug out [my boy]
lay her to rest with dignity
cover her
throw the last handful of soil
with single tear
then press the mound with the back of my
little plastic spade
crouched
with a satisfying sand castle pat
or will her fingers and hand push through
with menacing strings playing
with each "hello young lady"
jolted back to life, Frankenstein's Bride
with soiled face, second hand wig,
and those compromise calottes I wore
at Lee Mitchels wedding \ all scragged

II

She is still there \ Not in biceps \ But lips \Not in shaven
head\ but shaven legs \Not in sleeved Tampax\but bitter
cramps- syncing with moon \ Not swagger \ But pay
grade \ Not bloke banter \ But male gaze \ Not fastening
top shirt button \ But wearing a bra \ Not being afraid \
But crossing over \ Not in pints with the lads \ But in
being forced by one later \ in trying not to give a fuck \ in
taking a pill the morning after \ She's still there \ Not in
the mirror \ But the silhouette

III

should i

extract

]Her[

ejector seat?

\purge

tweezer teased \ splintered curve\ operate

remembering birthdays | with scalpel \careful

not to damage

grafted

tree

memories

draw out |

gentle touch? |

with salt

the kind one?

is that her?   a friend of daisies?

or\ bad memory?   bad tattoo?

her power tools??   I am not sure

is that it\   we part ways?

will i let in   water after i sieve

her & hang   her to dry? still

be waterproof?   do I say goodbye

now? or   return on a good

drying day \   unpeg her ....

she's strong?   I know that's her/

lugging round life   In an old battered

suitcase Up Parbold Hill like a knackered Wigan Sisyphus in case I
ever need to see what baggage I have/or open up \ She never says
no \ asks how you are\ doesn't complain\ not expected to\been
through a lot together\ friends forever? thanks for the memories?
but it's both of us /that hold up our fist/a]Feminist[with other
Women??{if they'll have me}\ or should i\ [coathanger] what's
left of me?shut the door?

28

\Part Two\ The Outside World

TWITTER IS MY DEADNAME

How would would you define a 'nonbinary' person? weirdo Absolutely disgraceful and mentally ill disgusting 😤😑😑 .trans aliens are NOT biological women or men!!! I will never ever, ever stop fighting this evil ideology that seeks to destroy us. There are 2 sexes only, go back to school to re-learn your biology! I won't use peope's pronouns for the same reason i won't talk to schizophrenics imaginary friends pronouns are Rohypnol

I mean this with the utmost respect, but it's gone too far tbh. Somebody who needs attention. Someone who doesn't understand biology. Attention seeking.

Confused. Broken and needs healing. gender is made up nonsense. Only bio logical sex is real. All you are is a fucking weirdo A man or a woman who you wants to feel special Be what you are and call yourself a girl/woman if have a vagina and a boy/man if you have a penis. Let's not complicate life. And none of that is real. Disturbed From Google:Mental disorder also called: mental illness A person who has zero to offer so they make up shit to feel special. People pretending to be something they are not and expecting everyone else to pretend with them. A man if they're male. A woman if they're female. Nonsense. Non-existent. Self -Worshipping Narcissist…No such thing people! Sorry but there is no such thing. This isn't a fairytale. your very normal non-conformity to sexist ste reotypes somehow makes you not the sex that you are is a quasi-rel igious belief that I have absolutely zero interest in persuading you out of. As I said you are welcome to believe in whatever you want to. I am also free to believe that those who pretend not to be the sex they are, are completely delusional and possibly rather attention seeking. Twitter is good for discourse such as this, even though I believe that such an inquiry not only is without any merit but also deserves no further inquiry. This inquiry stems from falsehood. That, imo, should be the end of it. what we may pretend to be. Schizoph enic…People pretending to be something th ey are not and expecting everyone else to pre tend with them. No matter how much you play with your mind you are a guy or a gal! No matter what we may pretend to be. In the scientific sense… someone who is not capable of being a complete person…Non-existent

MY LITTLE DOLL

Butch doll
glorious macho doll
Hard as nails doll\ talking out
the side of its mouth\ doll\ with
a ciggy on\ doll\ You swagger\
and you can doll your own
with the best of them\ O\ Oh!
dolls been talking to action man\
and they've just bit the pin off the grenade\
and spat it out\ Not long now\ You're all doll this\
an doll that\ like a doll/ A kick arse machete of a doll
Not Dolled up to the nines but giving the biggest Ken
in the place a piggy back\ or squaring up to them\
just for a laugh \ Just to show they were doll enough
Just in case anyone thought they were a doll for a minute
You can doll it out \ but you can't take it Like a doll \ on your
chin\ Who the   [DOLL]   do you think you are? Doll!
Are you fucking dolling me ? < < You can take the doll
out of Wigan but you can't take Wigan out the doll??
Hey doll\ you don't have any [nipples] \ which is as it
should be \ Did you scratch them off in puberty?
Rag doll's just a bundle of pollyanna knots
+ Tovarishch Matryoshka\ the russian doll
< does well to hide [inside itself] <
Sinks deep\shame deep\layer deep
Oh god\ I drank one to many dolls
last night - drunk on dolls
swimming-drowning in dolls
'Can you pay by doll?'
I do, every day \

HOW TO BUILD A ROAD WE WALK ON TOGETHER
After Cunto (Preface, penultimate paragraph)

wind whipped up again < dandelions ripped from roots < sky
darkens < twitter birds storm \ murmurate the sun < through
the cloud \ Cassimera's / orange beret marmalades through
ashen streets / our lantern shining the way / you are zest/
The old road is paved with matted wigs/ cheap size 9   golden
heels / a [clause 28] banner/ a womens disco /the tombstone
Aids advert/ thousand of boring / meetings / a life saving / >>
switchboard /and a shit tonne of glitter/ Leo's hand stubbles
their clipped neck=Thats my hand too, we run towards the
road as we are old enough to remember it<A fire breaks out
melting the tarmac!\ Choking, the apologetic 'honestly any
will do'enby at the pronoun go round, grabs a bucket ^puts it
out^ Behind the smoke >Beck's Beanie is bringing it at butch
points bingo > their voice is a gifted path / i follow /Day your
life IS the poem/ your words are footsteps .   . . .I stand in
them /no eye-contact kettlebell-king changes in the [shower
cubicle] at the gym \ > gives me the nod / just once, which
is enough / Cos I've got their back/ Clairey's bitten tongue a
pothole but we spit out her blood and patch it up.   D a n ' s
honey soothes the pain > Ro's tash is a street sign , Marcey's
potato milk> the white dashed line, Alina's mycelial network
runs beneath the cobbles, Ollie spots the unnameable horror
blocking the way, but Benjmina climbs us to safety. Mel your
spirit fires up our engine and we all jump on the back of an
open air bus\ but we become the [tourist attractions] we are
crammed over the sides\ a string of us flying in the wind daisy
chained. SHAR our conductor/ orchestrates the route, Beth
narrowly misses evicting her own body but we pull her on

board. Brendan is the driver with no license, he cooks pasta from the steering wheel, Lynne's executive realness proceeded drag race, Jo's eyes are our headlights powered by shock. But we are on the move, together. Our destination is already behind us. rolled up sleeves falling out of reach. Deadname and pervert arrows come slurring in from all directions. Joelle who's seen worse stands in the way protects us all with her tweed jacket which is made of impenetrable wool made of butch dykes and truth threads woven from aspic and leather. Delusional, predatory grenades try to land but the drag queens shield them with their fake tit breast plates. The weather takes a turn for the worse, misinformation rains down, like broken toilet cisterns, some of us jump off the bus to take cover. It starts snowing, which is bad because we are the snowflakes! A white blanket pervades our way, and we lose sight of the road, start to pansy off course. But it's ok, we grit the road with all the salt from our tears. In the distance we see egyptian fags, our brothers, battered down dark alleys, entrapped by Apps. We hold our breath> weightless we float through the Polish LGBT Free Zone, invisible. Way down the road we hard shoulder a stop at Chechnya, South Africa, Kenya, Saudi Arabia and all the other graveyards < pray for safe passage grabbing two of each queer ever known. Our bus/ an arc, we paddle for dry land. And crushed together we are Prided face to face, breathing the same glitter crossing all borders at the same time, we are a satellite, a planet, tomorrow/yesterday, a moon coming out. Sailing in the damp pitch silk, and sibling beacons sparkle from ashore so we never run aground.
Are always proud.

PROUD WEED?...SOMETIMES

Just as I
finally
become
valid
to myself
I find I'm not
to
others
Like
The
Far right
Like
An equality
Institution
Like
The
Bots
on twitter
I
Need more
Time
To be
Converted
In case I hurt
The woman
In me
But
I'm telling you
I don't want to hurt
The woman
In me
It doesn't
Feel
Like you are
Protecting
Me
The
Woman
Or
The
Other
Was this just
A
Ghost
Or
Echo
Then
In the
Machine
Back
To
Dissolving
My fizzy
Daily effervescent tablet
Swallowing...
I came so close
Could taste
The grass
But
Roundup
Has sprayed
Me away
To only
Leave
Mono
Culture
I'm a proud
Weed
Though
Only just
Was a
Trans(parent)
One
Before
Help
I can
Feel the conversion
Happening
I am
Disappearing
Again

flowers, each are a distinct individual.
The flower is made of multiple miniature
These are known as ray florets.
It opens when the sun rises and
clamps up when the sun sets.
Dandelion can be an allergen for some people.
However, its pollen is not an allergen.
They are also called ruderal or pioneer
plants as they are usually the first
plants that colonizes.
disturbed land
(like land after a wildfire)
With their golden flowers in the early spring,
dandelions represent the return of life.
the rebirth of growth and green after a harsh winter
with bright yellow flowers symbolising
optimism, growth, and good luck.
In addition to granting wishes.
many people believe that dandelion seeds
to loved ones when you blow
will carry your thoughts and dreams
them into the air. It's been said that
if you can blow all the seeds off a
dandelion with a single breath, then
the person you love will love you back.
Dandelions are considered a weed. Weeds are always under threat.
Dandelions represent 3 different
celestial bodies at 3 different
phases of their life. The plant's
Yellow flower represents the sun.
Really, the dispersed seeds look like the stars.
Finally, the puffy dandelion ball
bears a resemblance to the moon.

0110

00000000000000000000000
00000000001000000000000
00001000001000000100000
00000100001000001000000
00000010001000010000000
00000001001000100000000
00111111111111111111100
00000000011100000000000
00000001001100000000000
00000010001100100000000
00000100001100001000000
00001000011110000100000
00000110000000011000000
00011000000000000110000
00100000000000000000100
10000000000000000000001
10000000000000000000001
11000000000000000000011
01100000000000000000110
00110000000000000001100
00001000000000000010000
00000110000000001100000
00000000111111110000000

Non Binary alphabet

0 = female

1 = male

010 = A = 0

b=1

c =01

d=10   e= 00   f= It spells escaping the binary

36

DETERMINING SEX IS NOT STRAIGHT FORWARD

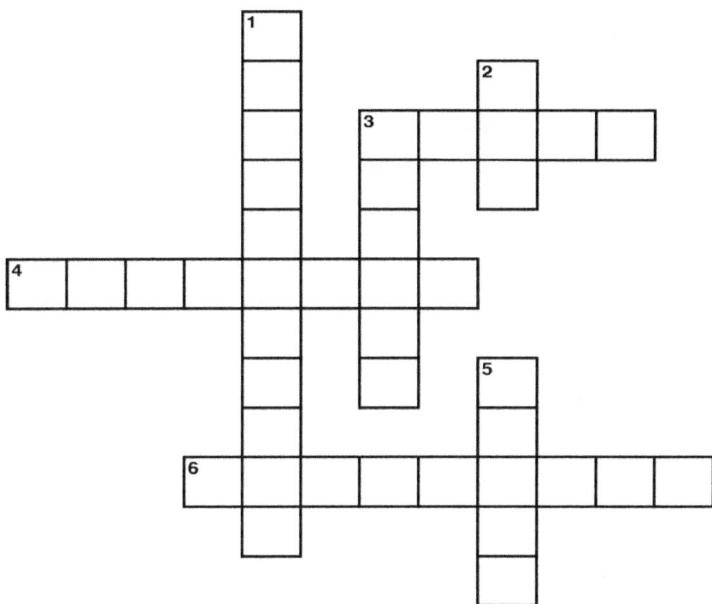

Across

[3] These chapters gave me teeth to grind a strong jawline at night just like my Dad. My mum's small waist worries if I'll ever find out (see title)(5)

[4] Messengers / juggle [hot [blood] sweats] with a deep hairy voice. (8)

[6] On the outside... - How Doctors determine fate. (7)

Down

[1] Instruction manuals come in two by two(11)

[2] Carrying a whole library everywhere you go is a heavy burden (3)

[3] A cell that lives in lust, text books or Twitter (6)

[5] What is not black and white matters - Life experience can change everything, even DNA here! (5)

Solutions on page 52

ANATOMY OF AN AFAB NON BINARY INDIVIDUAL
Figure 1

Brain - Is this where all the problems started? ------------------------------------

Lips - female presentation\\ soft\ sensual\tender but words are
spit bricks building bravados of fist kisses -------------------------------------

Breasts - male gaze, dysphoria darks, may contain traces of objectification
and lived experience if allergy present, if the sight knocks you sick. ---------

Nipples - puberty scarred<but not healed reveal [scratched off event]. ------
Do they still work? IN THE EVENT OF CHILD REARING -
PULL CHORD Ie. do they leak deep worries or milk? Too big,
too pink, too there.

Wrists - Fem little snaps. A key factor in misgendering. ---------------------
Nails - Clipped short neutral fashion - as per dyke presentation. -------------

Sex Identifier - The doctor determines a sex from this. So can a -------------
verdict be pleasure?

Knee (Grazed) - chronic injury as diagnosed in Tomboy Time dated
between the ages of 4 and an indistinguishable time during puberty. ----------
It's a state of mind. (see brain DNA - Junk DNA) = dark matter.

Hesitant Armpit and Leg Hair - failing to conform to male or
female accepted presentation. ---

Mammalian Gametes - because Twitter

IS IT WORTH IT?

problem<
being ENBY<
MISGENDERED.
Never pass<
Always
fail<
GENDER
BINARY REINFORCED
UNLESS DON'T leave house <
look at   phone<watch tv < read books<
Wash   hair<go on internet<wear   most
of your<   clothes>EXCEPT THAT TOP   that fits
just right   <or look in mirror-you can go a   whole day
without   being misgendered. **At being YOU**<
On average we get misgendered 30 times
a day (i just made that up because how can you
count?)) so that's 210 times a week, 10,920 times a year.
So in a lifetime that's... LOADS If you get told you are male/
female that many times and you still feel different...There has got
to be something in that right???? I checked the ONS* and it said Life exp

ectancy   at birth
in UK   was 79
for   males
& 82.9   for
females;   Life
expectancy   for ENBY
is un-   known
are we   kettled
ghosts   then? only
real at   sunset?
or through two way   mirrors when questioned

*[office for National Statistics]

Waiting times

We are ~~currently booking appointments~~ for people who ~~were referred to the service in July 2018. The longest wait time is currently 62 months as of September 2023. We~~ are ~~currently booking~~ transfer ~~of care from August 2021 as of September 2023 and further transfer of care referrals are~~ in process ~~to be added to our waiting list. (This information was last checked,~~ reviewed and updated ~~on 18 September 2023)~~ Individual ~~waiting times are variable and unfortunately we cannot give specific times for individual waits. Please do not contact the clinic to enquire about waiting times as~~ we cannot ~~provide any more information than is provided within this section.If you have received confirmation that your referral has been~~ accepted we will ~~not~~ remove you ~~from the list. Please keep us updated of any changes to your contact details.~~

*taken from Porterbrook Clinic Website Sept 2023, one of eight gender identity clinics in the UK.

PART 3: A NON-BINARY HEROIC CROWN

The following poem is a collaboration piece.

I contacted as many non-binary people I knew and asked them to tell me what it feels like for them to be non-binary/gender queer and to write that down, briefly and in whatever form they liked. A line, a paragraph, a page, a poem, a stream of consciousness. One piece I received was a voice message.

Once I received enough responses, I worked on each individual response, apart from Alina's sonnet which we wrote together. I tried to amplify and interrogate the essence of their words and for each person I created a 14 line sonnet. The final line of the first sonnet was then repeated in the first line of the second (and so on) linking the sonnets together. Some of the repeated lines are not repeated exactly but have queered to meet the next sonnet. Characteristically not quite fitting the rules or boundaries. One of the responses, from Leo felt so similar to part of my experience that I mirrored our sonnets. The final form is 14, connected 14 line sonnets finished by the final 15th master sonnet built from the repeated lines that thread the poem and people together. The structure celebrates the differences and unique experience as well as reflects our shared similarities of being non-binary in the 2020's. It is a celebration, an archive and a poetic unison that I hope gives people an insight into the endless facets of being Non-binary, Gender queer, Gender free, of being human.

EVA

I know nothing about planting >yet

> my gender is a garden

Frosted underground bulbs \ lie

& thin Winter cloaks

I am No address < no flowers sent

The only real is taken from birds in dreams >

>notes \ I am a gap gasping

I wish for wisp > Wanting

To escape gaze < eyes on stalks <

Fruiting silent chambers

Sealing my sex \

Wax \ rinding fallow

ground \ coordinates scattered not sewn

I am wind - only part of the weather

ALINA

I am rain - only part of the weather.

Unusual how

water becomes less dense when frozen - how

capillary action pulls water up not down - how

tiny triangular shapes pull close - push away - how

water becomes the measure of all things; our 0, our 100 - how

a paper clip floats on water, only when supported by a sheet of

paper - how

water is already burnt so cannot burn - how

closely I hold you because we are not charged the same - how

one drop is one drop but many is a deluge - how

some rain is dry - how

one side pulls close and the other pulls back - how

one drop is a warning but a shower a blessing - how

one is not one is not one

SAMMY

If one is not one is not one
if now remembers always
can always not forget
if i look long enough
can I see myself whole
if I shout loud enough can i
yesterday a response
can I occasion the future
if I adventure young .... enough
can I return my youth
if i love nimbly enough
can i bind hatred
if all hatred relies on erasing
can i paint myself true

BETH

can i paint myself true
not her
a label fail fathomed
stitched up liminal thread
history of
recipe batched out
head down pay-gapped
processed white bread but I'm
still whole with all my ribs
before a man's story stole one
and buried it with my likeness
i'm in the Garden muddy
making pies of myself
i am my own food

DAY

I am my own food>

a verb > fucking ^ or ironing _

I am still | moving >

I am sacred >changing

I am a temporary life >living

I am not myself - a star imploding

I am queerness, queering

I am the door left Ajar >opening

I am opportunity

I am just maybe pondering I am

a question mark thinking one day! I don't know perhaps

potentially we'll see

THEY try to noun me \ weaponise vulnerable ~~label~~< target me

but by the time they've defined me

in their sights I'm already flying

RORY

Am I already flying?

far...side-body through velvet- shoulder on midriff

Another's pleasure as my own?

geometry of pubes when I tuck.

glad for my tautness, from tail to tip; Yet

ask me about girlhood,

it pours out of my face and

Patriarchy<which I am riddled < unthinkably colossal.

I don't know what I am, is it time to unfurl?

feel my way into this world.

hamster rolls; ballroom holds; head-to-head,

making pillows of chests.

counter-balanced body > weighted right

I only speak of things discovered

DAN

I discovered speak

Listening to the sea inside -waving

Much too far out

Always - but still

I wash my single self ashore

sailing for all to see

an island that only exists twice a day

Like Hilbre - a bust-ed clock

That you can walk to.

If u visit at the right time

My selkie ship is ours - has no rudder

Pushed by sun-Pulled by moon

Floating - open

BECK

Floating, sinking <

< swallow < [madam] at the supermarket

[Young lady] by your dad

Excuse me [miss, her name is, come on missus, hey queen]

weighted words pulling

body will always betray

worth it flu because your voice became so deep

take up [less space fit small place]

in cracks be mistaken

dive down, curves

throwing up thin enough

flat enough, waif, wished Boi enough

being underwater for too long its

breaking the surface when you've already drowned

MARZENA

Breaking	Surface
My Chicago bred	polish queer
between culture	across border
too queer	not queer enough
Too immigrant	not immigrant enough
too eastern european	too american
too working class	too inbetween
undocumented	handsome intersectioned
myth shattering	identity fluxed
Ass	don't kiss no
fit box	fit binary
Forget	history
erase yourself	dominant reality
I grew out my box	and built a new world

OLLIE

I grew out of what I was taught
People I should respect
line up monolith to poke me
into Right pose
I was taught
[man-made chrysalis]
a size too small.
I was taught
but when they crave pattern
I see chaos
strip each layer
Left bare in my beauty
I dropped the obligation
Like vowels or leaves, became butterfly butch

MARCY

Like vowels or leaves
like the   <thing> in between the words.
Like 'i can't be assed with gender'
google told me I have to spell it like 'arsed'
when i realised you don't actually have to capitalise words
i never looked back >
my queerness is > several tabs open
including 'what are judith butlers' pronouns' and
'cheap weighted hula hoop'
people tell me it's spelled 'woman'
my They is autocorrected to She.
they can autocorrect all they want \whine about my spelling
but im dyslexic, and i'm not assed
i'm nonbinary however you wanna spell it

LEO

however you spell it I'm Leo
small step Scuff knee tomboy tat lad
plain view Camouflage circa 1978
Section 28\promo cover boi crushed
small town \Wrong toilets \flushed
walking in bent boots\ gravity shoes
tread two option tick box blues\
self\swallowed sunken street
grasped missing yardstick
found / strutted feet blistered
million miles trek /cuffed
back time > peeled to proud
They had always been here

JAY

had They always been here?
proud to peel back time
cuffed million miles trek
blistered feet strutted / found
missing yardstick /grasped
self swallowed sunken street
tread two option tick box blues\
walking in bent boots\ gravity shoes
small town \Wrong toilets \flushed
Section 28\promo cover boi crushed
plain view Camouflage circa 1973
small step Scuff knee tomboy tat lad
however you spell it I'm Jay

KI

However you call it - If I was called boy first
i would have been Hezekia
great grandad's feet teeting my first steps
if I was Hezekia first >I would have been a first choice
if I was Kiah, which I was
i would have been girl, second
doctor said 'it is a girl'
but auntie said she's the spit
if I would have been different on the outside
they would see Hezekiah taking breaths
his smile on my lips/ his ears/ passed on/ listening
his old eyes seeing the world fresh
what i saw was Ki
i had my own birth

US

We are wind - only part of the weather

one is not one is not one

Can we paint ourselves true

We are our own food

in their sights we're already flying

We only speak of things discovered

Floating - open

breaking the surface when we've already drowned

We grew out of our [box] and built a new world

of voweled leaves /butterfly butch

non-binary however you wanna spell it

We have always been here

however you call it

We had our own birth.

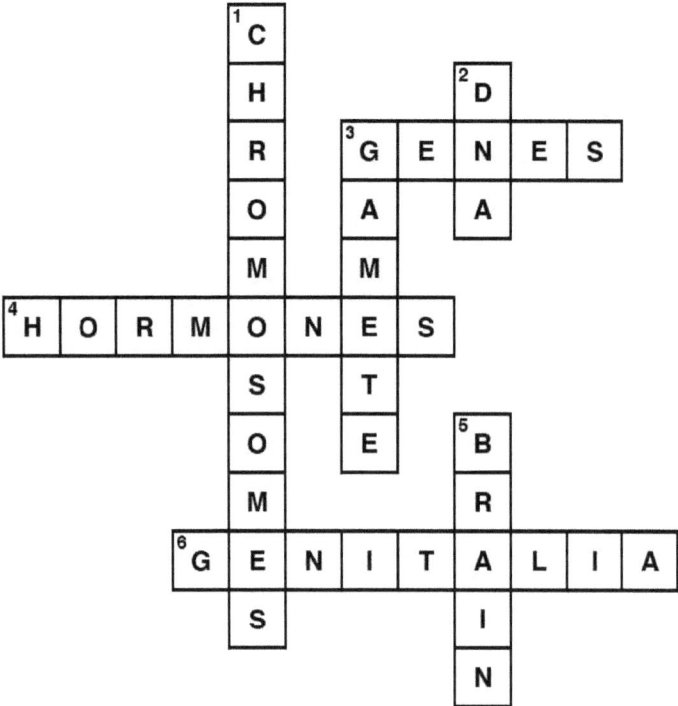

ACKNOWLEDGEMENTS

To Queer Bodies @queerbods for being an amazing groundbreaking poetry collective. Day Mattar for giving amazing skillful notes on so many of the poems. For teaching me what poetry is. For telling me straight, honestly and from your heart. Brendan Curtis for believing in me, encouraging me, for mentoring, for your brilliant mind and ideas. You are my valued friends, first and always mentors, and the world is a better place for having you both. Rachael Brackenridge and Lou PlazzyBag for the inspiration to start. To Kae Tempest for inspiration. To Creative Future for giving me confidence and providing a platform for underrepresented voices. Lovely Word Poetry for their brilliant poetry nights and Slams. To Lynne Harwood for reading my poems, and giving great notes. Leandros for encouragement, Mike for validation and Beck for belief. Elinor Randle for helping transform many of the poems in this book onto their first stage appearance. To Claire Bigley for seeing potential in my work as a touring entity, and continued encouragement.

For my fellow Non-Binary Heroic Crown contributors: you truly are my Heroes, braving the world as yourself in the face of daily denial. Without your amazing, honest, radical, unique words the poem would not exist. In many ways your original text is more precious. Massive thanks to Aaron Kent for his insightful editing, skillful and brilliant writing and tireless coordination of @BrokenSleepBooks. I am so proud to be part of this radical, inspiring and vital Press. To Joelle Taylor for your help, kindness, belief, brilliance, words and wisdom, this book would not reach the world without you.

LAY OUT YOUR UNREST

www.ingramcontent.com/pod-product-compliance
Lightning Source LLC
LaVergne TN
LVHW041237080426
835508LV00011B/1257